J612
MER

FEB - 2 2012

THE LIFE CYCLE OF A

HUMAN

By Robin Merritt

Published by The Child's World®
1980 Lookout Drive
Mankato, MN 56003-1705
800-599-READ
www.childsworld.com

The Child's World®: Mary Berendes, Publishing Director
The Design Lab: Kathleen Petelinsek, design
Red Line Editorial: Editorial direction

ISBN: 978-1-60973-147-2
LCCN: 2011927735

Printed in the United States of America
Mankato, MN
July 2011
PA02089

3 9082 11659 9385

TABLE OF

CONTENTS

Life Cycles...4

Humans...7

Infancy...8

Childhood...16

Adolescence...20

Adulthood...23

New Infants...27

Life Cycle Diagram...30

Web Sites and Books...32

Glossary...32

Index...32

LIFE CYCLES

Every living thing has a life cycle. A life cycle is the steps a living thing goes through as it grows and changes. Humans have a life cycle. Animals have a life cycle. Plants have a life cycle, too.

A cycle is something that happens over and over again. A life cycle begins with the start of a new life. It continues as a plant or creature grows. And it keeps going as one living thing creates another, or **reproduces**—and the cycle starts over again.

A human's life cycle has several steps: from an egg a human grows and changes into an adult.

Humans, dogs, and other animals have life cycles.

The only **mammal** to always walk on two legs is a human.

HUMANS

Humans are mammals, like elephants, dogs, and mice. Mammals have many traits in common. Fur or hair covers parts of their bodies. And they give birth to live babies instead of laying eggs. Mammal mothers also **nurse** their young.

Like all mammals, humans are warm-blooded. This means their body temperature stays about the same, whether it is hot or cold outside. Most land mammals walk on four legs. Humans are the only mammals that always walk on two legs.

INFANCY

A newborn human is called an infant. Usually each mother has one infant at a time, though sometimes twins or even triplets are born. Most infants start to cry as soon as they are born. Crying fills their lungs with air.

Infants immediately need their parents to take care of them. Since they cannot speak, crying tells adults when infants need attention.

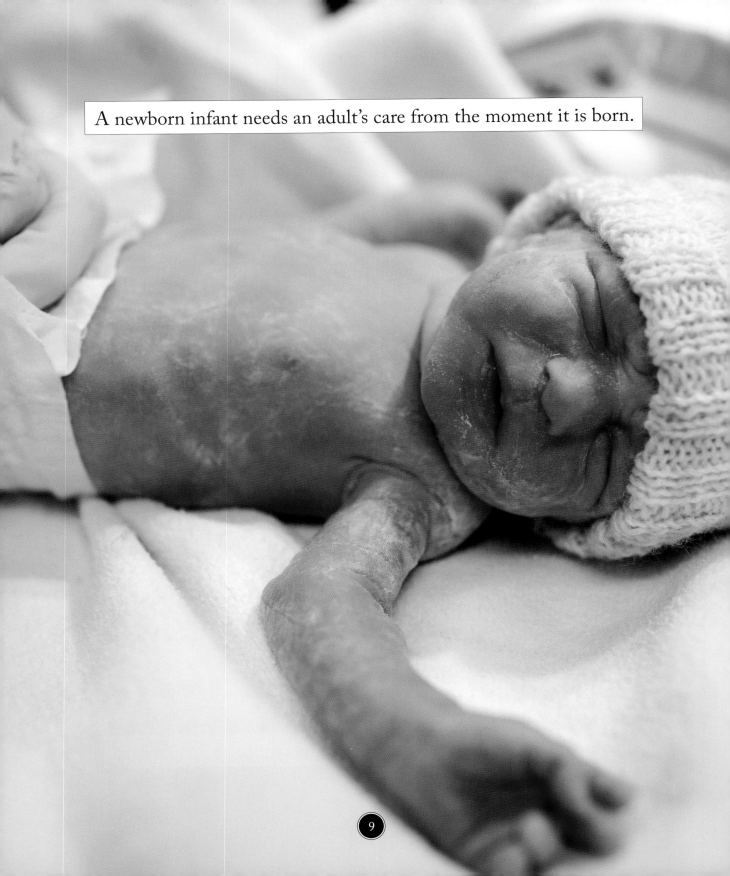

A newborn infant needs an adult's care from the moment it is born.

Infants are only fed human milk or formula for their first months.

Infants are born without teeth. They get the nutrients they need by drinking milk for the first months of their lives. Some infants nurse milk from their mothers' bodies. Other infants are fed baby formula, which is milk made just for human babies. Drinking cow's milk upsets an infant's stomach.

Infants need adults to take care of them in other ways, too. Mothers and fathers keep them warm by dressing them and giving them shelter from rain and cold. Infants can wiggle their arms and kick their legs, but they cannot walk. They can't even lift their heads at first. Parents must carry their babies around and hold their heads in place.

At first, infants sleep a lot. They need about 16 hours of sleep each day. When they are awake they are usually eating, crying, cuddling with mom or dad, or watching their surroundings. Each moment infants are awake, they are learning about the world around them.

An infant cries to get his parent's attention.

13

An infant usually begins crawling in her first year.

14

Infants grow quickly during their first year of life. A 7-pound (3-kg) infant may weigh 21 pounds (9.5 kg) at the end of her first year. That is three times her birth weight!

Infants learn to sit up on their own and crawl. They begin to pick up objects and play with them. By the end of their first year infants may say simple words, like "mama" or "dada." They usually grow two to four front teeth and begin to eat different foods. Bananas and mashed sweet potatoes make good meals for infants this age.

CHILDHOOD

After their first birthdays, humans are often called toddlers. They are just learning to walk, or toddle. As toddlers grow, they start to learn to do many things for themselves. They can move on their own. They can also pick up food or use a spoon to eat.

Children continue to grow quickly. They run and jump and can soon throw a ball. Children learn to play with other children. They put puzzles together or use blocks to build towers. They learn to talk and express their feelings. Playing with other children lets them practice ways to understand each other.

A toddler can kick a ball and play.

17

Children can eat adult foods as they get more teeth.

18

Children grow two sets of teeth during childhood. They will continue to get baby teeth until they are three years old. As children get more teeth, they can eat the same foods as adults. Meat, vegetables, and fruit can be easily eaten. Many children lose all of their baby teeth by age 12. A full set of adult teeth replaces them.

ADOLESCENCE

Around age 12, humans enter **adolescence**. This is a time when children begin to mature into adults. Adolescents go through **puberty**. That means their bodies start to change and look more like adult bodies. During this time, human bodies become ready to reproduce.

Adolescents are more independent than children. Some might get jobs or learn to drive. But most still need their parents to give them a home, food, and other things. Humans take care of their young longer than any other mammals.

Human bodies change and grow as they go through adolescence.

When humans turn 18, many consider them to be adults.

ADULTHOOD

Most humans stop growing by age 18. Many people consider humans to be adults after that age. Adulthood is the longest part of the human life cycle. In the United States, women live to be about 79 and men live to be about 72. But many humans live longer than that. Some even live past 100!

Humans live longer than any other mammal. Diseases and accidents may shorten their lives, though.

Adults can take care of themselves and make their own decisions. They no longer need their parents to care for them. Some have their own families. Adults also have many responsibilities, such as jobs.

As humans get older, they start to show signs of **aging**. Their hair may start to turn gray. Some people develop wrinkles on their skin. Hearing can become difficult. And eyes may not see things as clearly as they did earlier in life.

As humans age, their hair often turns gray and wrinkles appear on their faces.

25

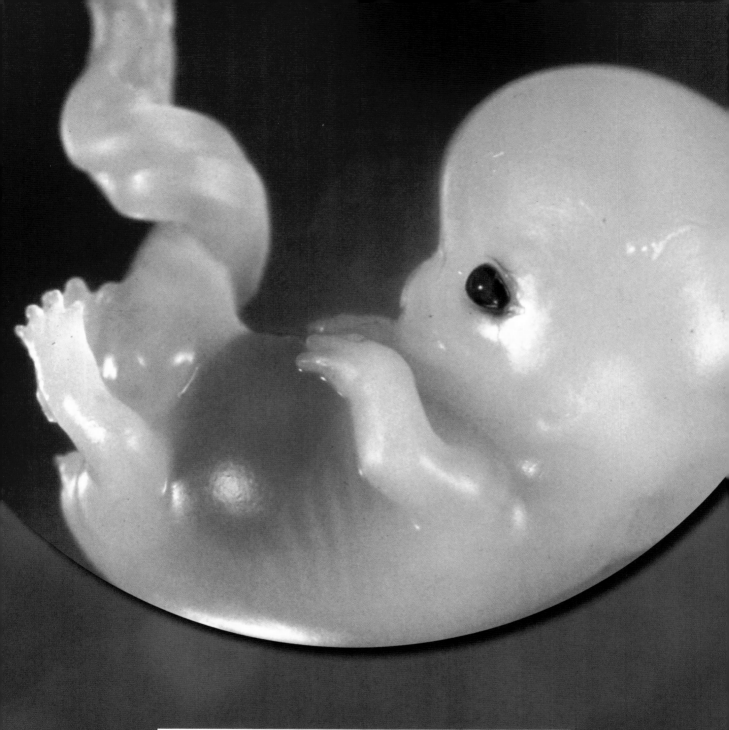

A human **embryo** grows inside a woman's **womb**.

NEW INFANTS

After puberty, men and women can reproduce. For most women, reproduction ends between ages 40 to 50. Men and women have **reproductive** cells. When these cells join inside a woman's body, her egg becomes **fertilized**. She becomes **pregnant**. The egg then grows into an embryo inside the mother's womb. At first, the embryo does not look very human.

As the embryo grows, it is fed nutrients through the mother's body. The food she digests and oxygen she breathes are passed through her blood to the embryo. There is no air in a mother's womb.

An embryo becomes a **fetus** as it grows. It looks more human each month. The fetus stays in the mother's womb for 40 weeks. By the last weeks, the fetus is ready to survive in the world.

A woman pushes the fetus out of her body and the infant is born. The womb's liquid leaves the infant's lungs. He can now breathe oxygen from the air. His parents will care for him for many years until he becomes an adult. The human life cycle continues.

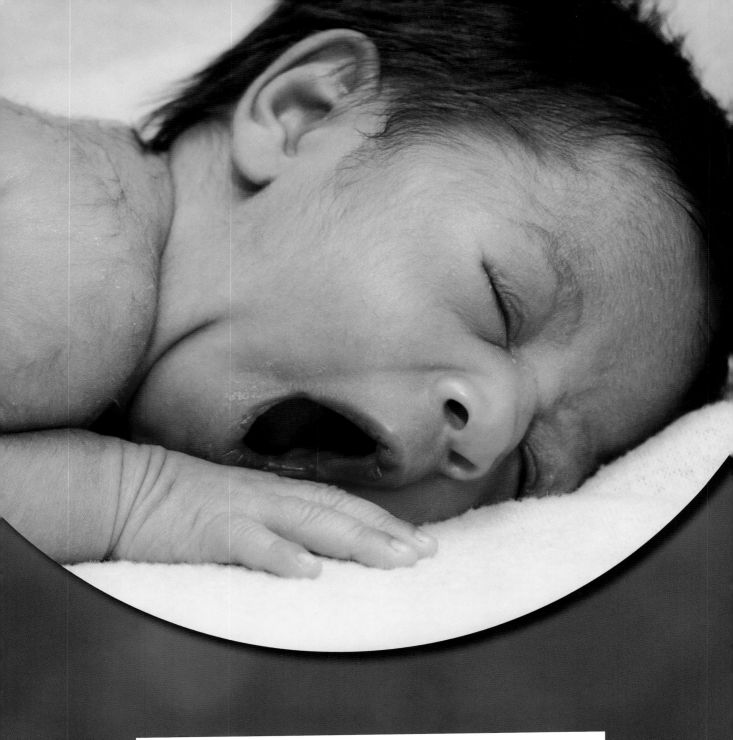

Newborn babies begin breathing air when they are born.

LIFE CYCLE DIAGRAM

Embryo grows into a Fetus in Womb

Infant

30

Adult

Adolescent

Child

31

Web Sites

Visit our Web site for links about the life cycle of a human: **childsworld.com/links**

Note to Parents, Teachers, and Librarians: We routinely verify our Web links to make sure they are safe and active sites. So encourage your readers to check them out!

Glossary

adolescence (ad-uh-LESS-unce): Adolescence is the time of life when a child develops into an adult. Humans enter adolescence around age 12.

aging (AY-jing): Aging is the process of becoming older. An aging human may have gray hair and wrinkles.

embryo (EM-bree-oh): An embryo is an organism in the early stages of growth. An embryo grows into a fetus.

fertilized (FUR-tuh-lyzd): Fertilized refers to an egg that can grow and develop into a new life. A fertilized egg soon becomes an embryo.

fetus (FEE-tuss): A human or other mammal begins life as an embryo and grows into a fetus before it is ready to be born. A human fetus grows in its mother's womb.

mammal (MAM-uhl): A mammal is a warm-blooded animal with hair or fur that makes milk for its babies. Human and whales are mammals.

nurse (NURSS): To nurse is to feed a young animal with milk from its mother's body. Many infants nurse from their mothers.

pregnant (PREG-nunt): A female is pregnant when she has an embryo or fetus inside her womb. A woman is usually pregnant for 40 weeks.

puberty (PYOO-bur-tee): Puberty is the time when a person's body changes from a child to an adult. Adolescents experience puberty.

reproduces (ree-pruh-DOOS-ez): If an animal or plant reproduces, it produces offspring. A human reproduces to continue the human life cycle.

reproductive (ree-pruh-DUCK-tiv): A reproductive cell or body part is used in making new creatures. Humans' reproductive cells combine to create new humans.

womb (woom): A womb is a hollow organ in a female mammal where her fetus or embryo can grow. A fetus grows in a woman's womb.

Books

Bellamy, Rufus. *The Human Lifecycle.* North Mankato, MN: Smart Apple Media, 2005.
Macnair, Dr. Patricia. *Life Cycle: Birth, Growth, and Development.* Boston: Kingfisher, 2004.
Prior, Jennifer. *The Human Life Cycle.* Huntington Beach, CA: Teacher Created Materials, 2005.

Index

32